GREAT F*CKING QUOTES

INSPIRATIONAL QUOTES AND AFFIRMATIONS TO MAKE YOUR DAY BRIGHT AS HELL

OLIVE MICHAELS

Copyright © 2023 by Sourcebooks
Cover and internal design © 2023 by Sourcebooks
Cover and internal design by Will Riley
Cover images © Emmanuel Avila/Pexels, Pat Whelen/Pexels
Internal images © Pexels, Pixabay, Unsplash, wirestock/Freepik

Sourcebooks and the colophon are registered trademarks of Sourcebooks.

Published by Sourcebooks, an imprint of Sourcebooks
P.O. Box 4410, Naperville, Illinois 60567-4410
(630) 961-3900
sourcebooks.com

Printed and bound in China.
PP 10 9 8 7 6 5 4 3 2 1

INTRODUCTION

Have you ever looked to an inspirational poster and felt let down?

Particularly in moments where you are more inclined to put a fist

through a wall than pause to observe an eagle soaring over a sunset.

Introducing *GREAT FUCKING QUOTES*, sayings that are so damn

inspiring that you can't help but feel uplifted and empowered! Don't

put a fist through a wall, raise it in fucking joy and power! With this

can't-miss collection, you've fucking got this!

You've got the power to look on the bright side of things and tell any **fuckers** who try to take you down to **get the fuck out of your light.**

KEEP YOUR FACE TO THE SUN,
AND IGNORE THAT *FUCKER* IN THE SHADOWS.

IF OPPORTUNITY DOESN'T KNOCK,

KICK OPEN THE GODDAMN DOOR.

What are you waiting for?

Get the fuck out there and make it happen.

You bet your ass you did. *Gold star day!*

I CAN
AND I ALREADY
FUCKING
DID.

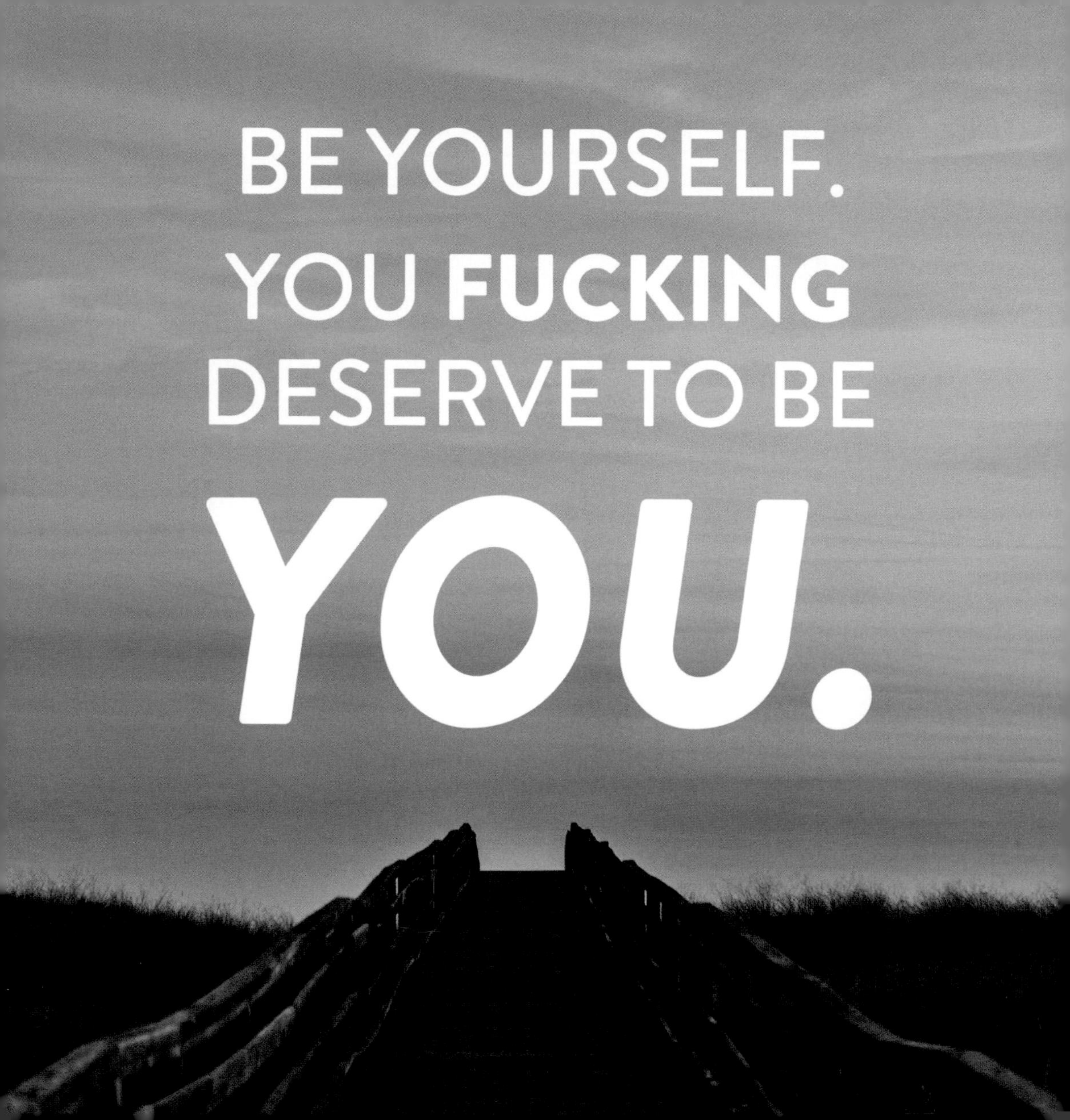
BE YOURSELF.
YOU **FUCKING**
DESERVE TO BE
YOU.

Live free and as **YOU** *want to.*

Don't answer to anyone.

You don't need to worry about what others are thinking. They are all hoping to be as **bitchin' awesome** as you are.

EVEN IF HOPE IS A THING WITH FEATHERS, **JUST CATCH THE DAMN THING.**

Waiting is a damn waste of time.
You know what you want, **so go out there
and get those fucking feathers.**

You're too badass to quit on yourself or your passions. **You can do fucking anything.**

QUITTING IS FOREVER, SO *GET OFF YOUR ASS AND GET IT DONE.*

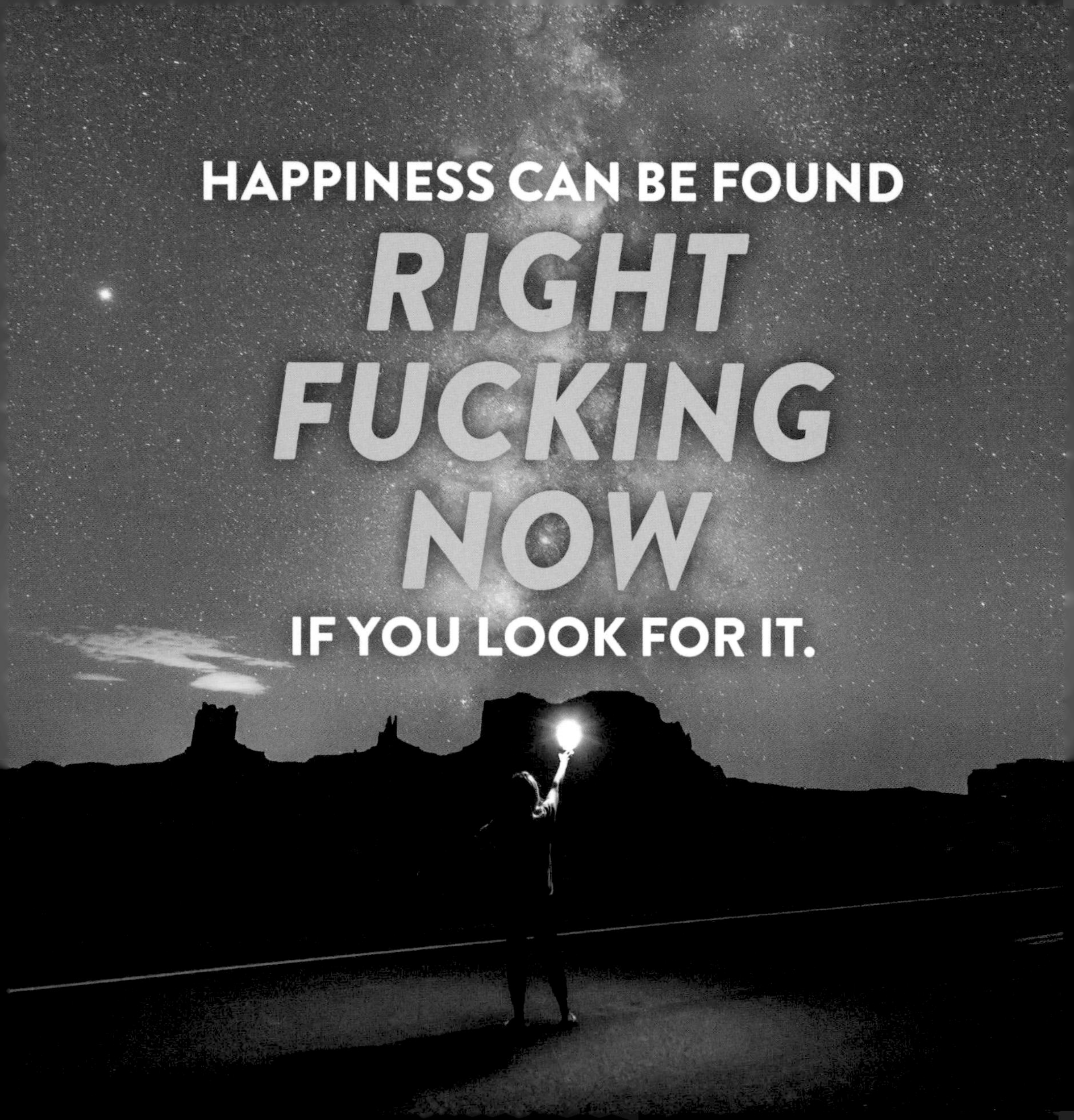
HAPPINESS CAN BE FOUND
RIGHT
FUCKING
NOW
IF YOU LOOK FOR IT.

You are free to choose whatever
the **fuck** makes you happy.
So what in the hell are you waiting for?

*When you feel intimidated, claim your power and sweetly tell that person to **fuck off**.*

THE NUMBER ONE SKILL IN LIFE
IS KNOWING WHEN TO SAY,

"I DON'T FUCKING THINK SO."

FOLLOW YOUR HEART, ESPECIALLY IF IT LEADS YOU TO COOL AS HELL PLACES. LIKE SKYDIVING.

THAT SHIT IS RAD AS HELL.

You know exactly what the hell you want in life, so what are you waiting for? Someone's lame-ass permission? **Fuck that.** You know what feels right for you.

It's wonderful to have so many great ideas.
So **what the hell** is stopping you
from taking action?

THINK.

THEN
FUCKING DO.

SOMETIMES
YOU GOTTA BE
THE RAINBOW FOR YOUR

OWN DAMN CLOUD.

You don't have to settle for a cloudy day. Shove those goddamn puffy things aside and **find your own damn rainbow.**

*Whining over what you missed out on will get you nowhere. **Quit your bitchin'** and rise to the challenge of tomorrow!*

YOU CAN'T TURN
BACK THE CLOCK,
BUT YOU CAN

SMASH
THE
FUCK
OUT OF IT.

*It's okay to know when you need a life change. You don't have to stay in one fucking place just to make some **asshole** happy.*

A positive start to your day
will get you through some nasty shit.

START YOUR DAY
WITH A LOUD
"*WHY THE
FUCK NOT?*"

HE WHO LAUGHS MOST *WILL GET THROUGH THIS SHITTY WEEK.*

It's not enough to chuckle these days.
*You need to **laugh your fucking head off.***

The pressure of everyone asking you to do things is a thing of the past.
Practice your "Fuck No" mantra.

GOOD THINGS
HAPPEN TO
THOSE WHO SAY,

"NO, I'M
FUCKING
BUSY."

*Trying out new ideas is nice, sure, but it's okay to throw a few things out the **fucking window** if they get in your way.*

You don't need a **fucking earthquake** to remind you how to appreciate each day.

FOR FUCK'S SAKE,

ENJOY THE LITTLE THINGS.

YOU FUCKING GOT THIS.

What's that lack of confidence shit
doing in your life? Your courage and power
are a **fucking vision to behold.**

Own your brightness. You have an inner light that **glows all over the fucking place.**

OF COURSE YOU
HAVE TO GO OUT
INTO THE DARK TO
SEE THE STARS.

*IT'S FUCKING
NIGHTIME.*

Have faith in your own
damn choices and decisions.

I THINK,

THEREFORE I'M
GODDAMN
AWESOME.

GET THE HELL OUT THERE

AND PUT YOUR BEST FOOT FORWARD.

*Sure, it's hard sometimes to start your day off right. So do it anyway and **get rid of that negative shit.***

There are a lot of things that can
get in the way of your goals.
Negativity is not a fucking option.

ERASE
ALL THAT
GODDAMN
NEGATIVITY
FROM YOUR
PLANS.

EVERY CLOUD HAS SOME KIND OF FUCKING LINING.

Sure there are problems, but every once in a while, **a goddamn positive thing** comes out of it.

Go one step further and show the whole
fucking world how **badass** you are.

BE THE
EXTRA IN

EXTRA-
FUCKING-
ORDINARY.

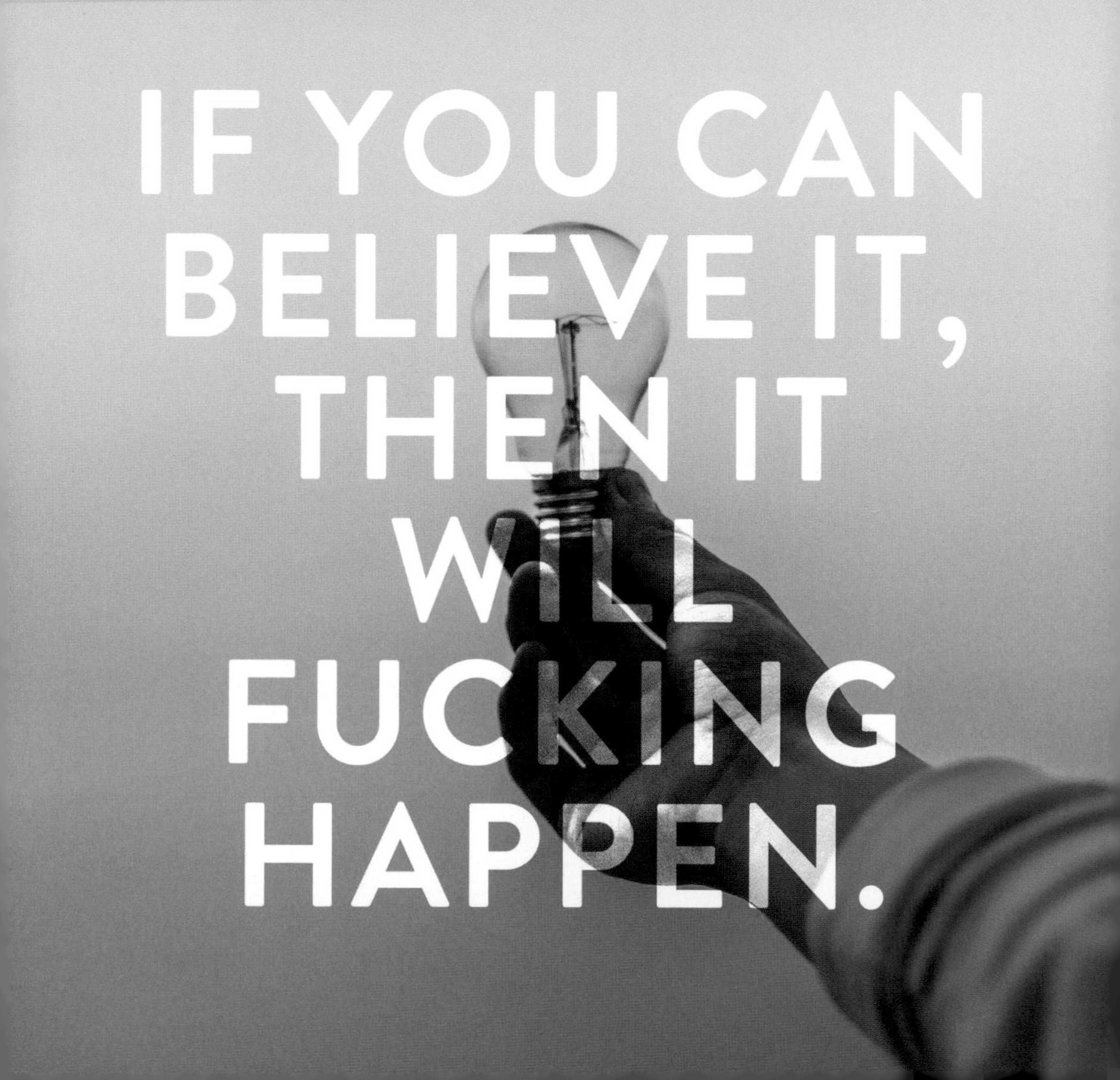
IF YOU CAN
BELIEVE IT,
THEN IT
WILL
FUCKING
HAPPEN.

The power of your mind is
fan-fucking-tastic.

Whatever you need in the morning
*to get the **fuck moving**, take it.*

COFFEE, YOU FUCKING COMPLETE ME.

DON'T POSTPONE YOUR OWN DAMN JOY.

*It's lovely to help others achieve their goals, but get **your ass moving** on your own damn happiness.*

Achievement comes in all shapes and sizes.
*They are all **fucking worthy.***

THE KEY TO SUCCESS IS
ANYTHING YOU FUCKING WANT IT TO BE.

*Following a plan is just dandy. It's also okay to say, **"Fuck that"** and jump to the finish line.*

*Even if you change your destination in life, you are still the **badass warrior** who got you there.*

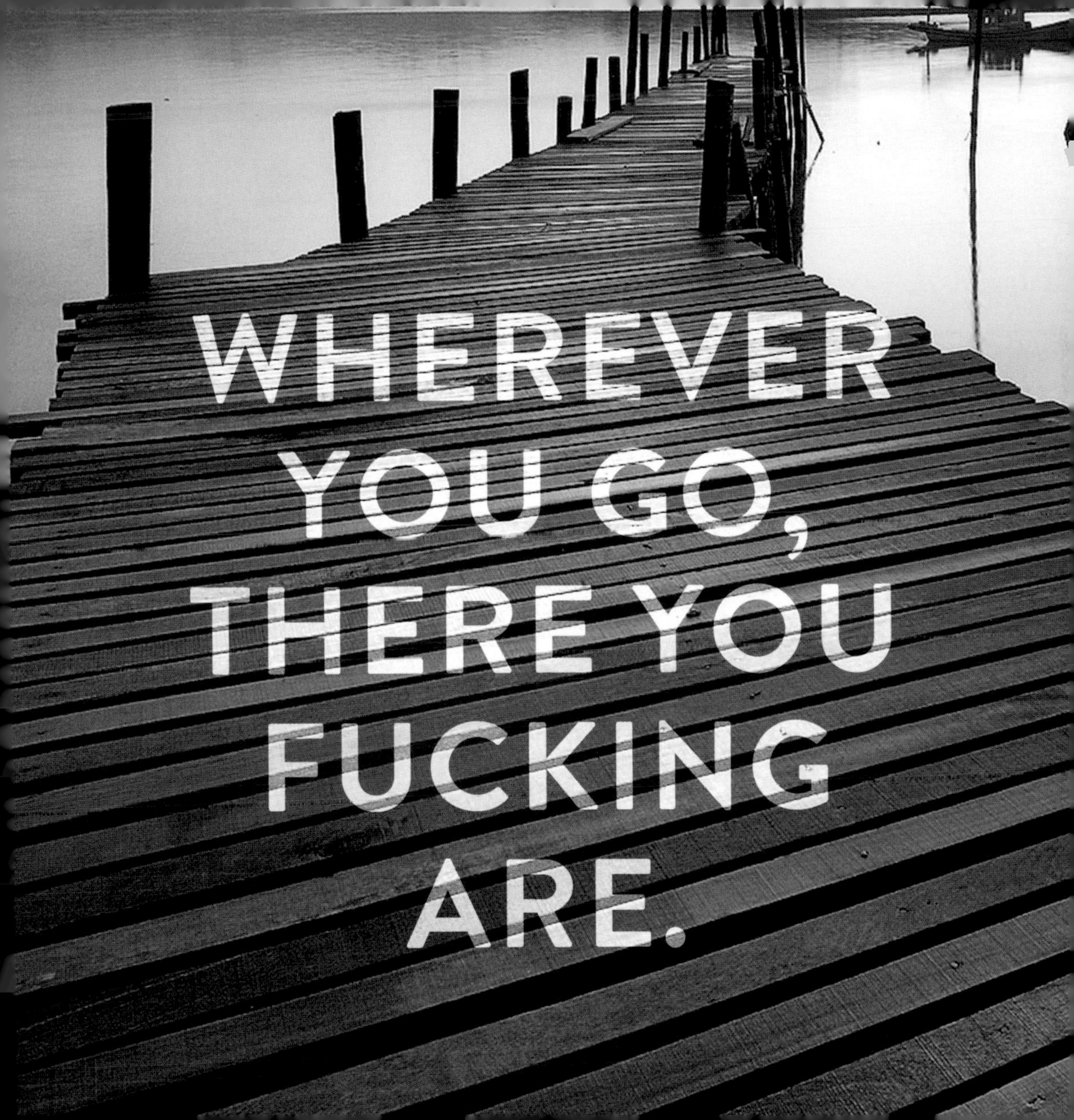
WHEREVER
YOU GO,
THERE YOU
FUCKING
ARE.

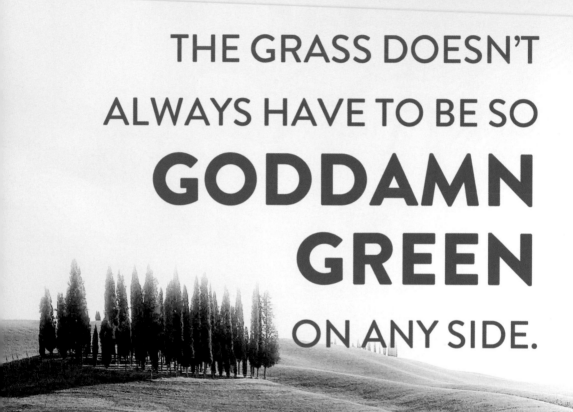

THE GRASS DOESN'T ALWAYS HAVE TO BE SO **GODDAMN GREEN** ON ANY SIDE.

*Striving for perfection or wishing for what others have isn't going to get you **a fucking star** on a sidewalk.*

Take that list of goals and start
*checking off those **damn boxes.***

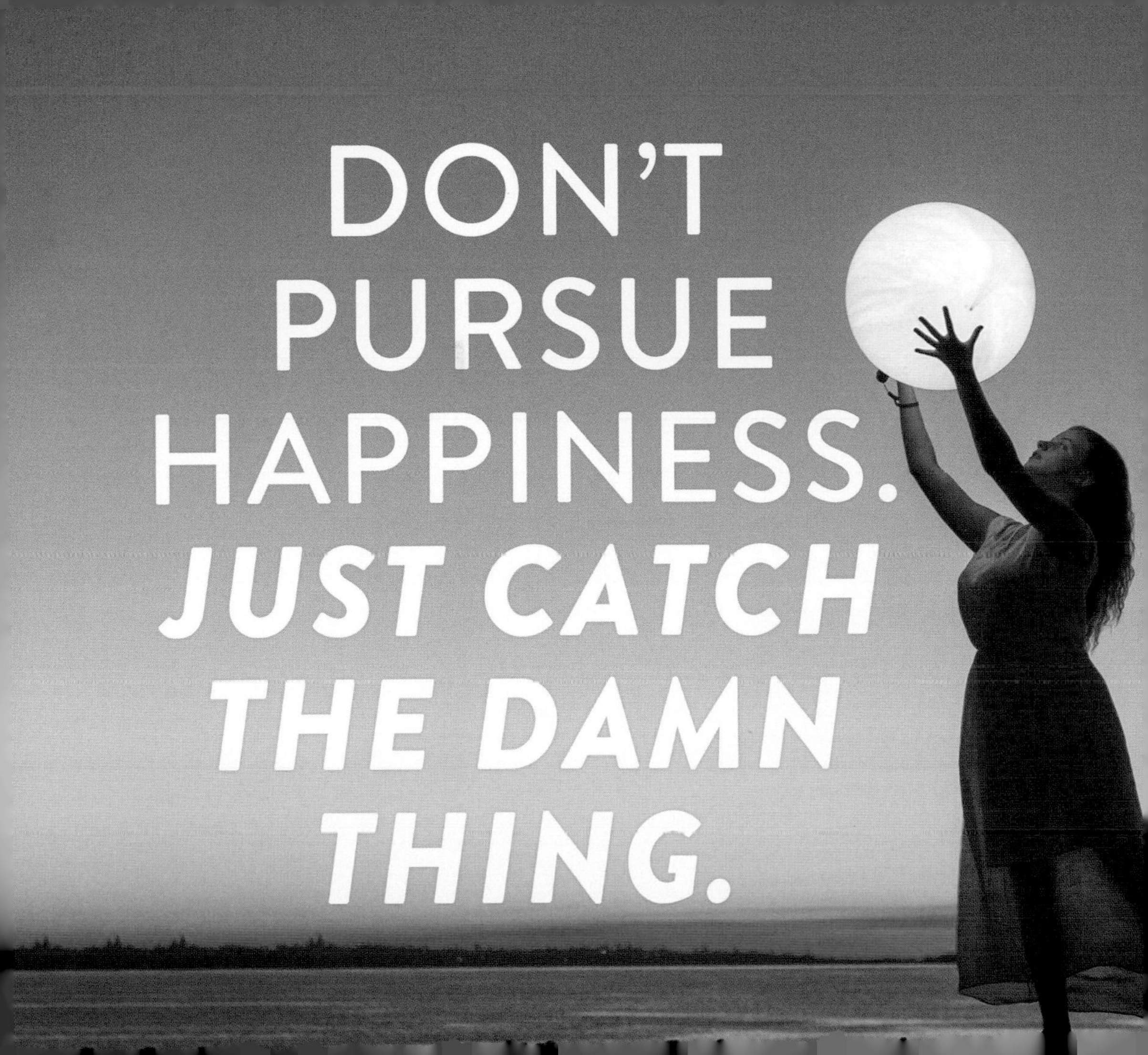
DON'T
PURSUE
HAPPINESS.
JUST CATCH
THE DAMN
THING.

THE APPLE
OF YOUR
EYE IS **YOU**,
BITCH.

*Learn to **fucking appreciate**
the gold that is you.*

For every goal you try, give yourself a
"Fuck Yeah" sticker.

YOU'RE NOT
A FUCKING
FAILURE IF
YOU TRIED.

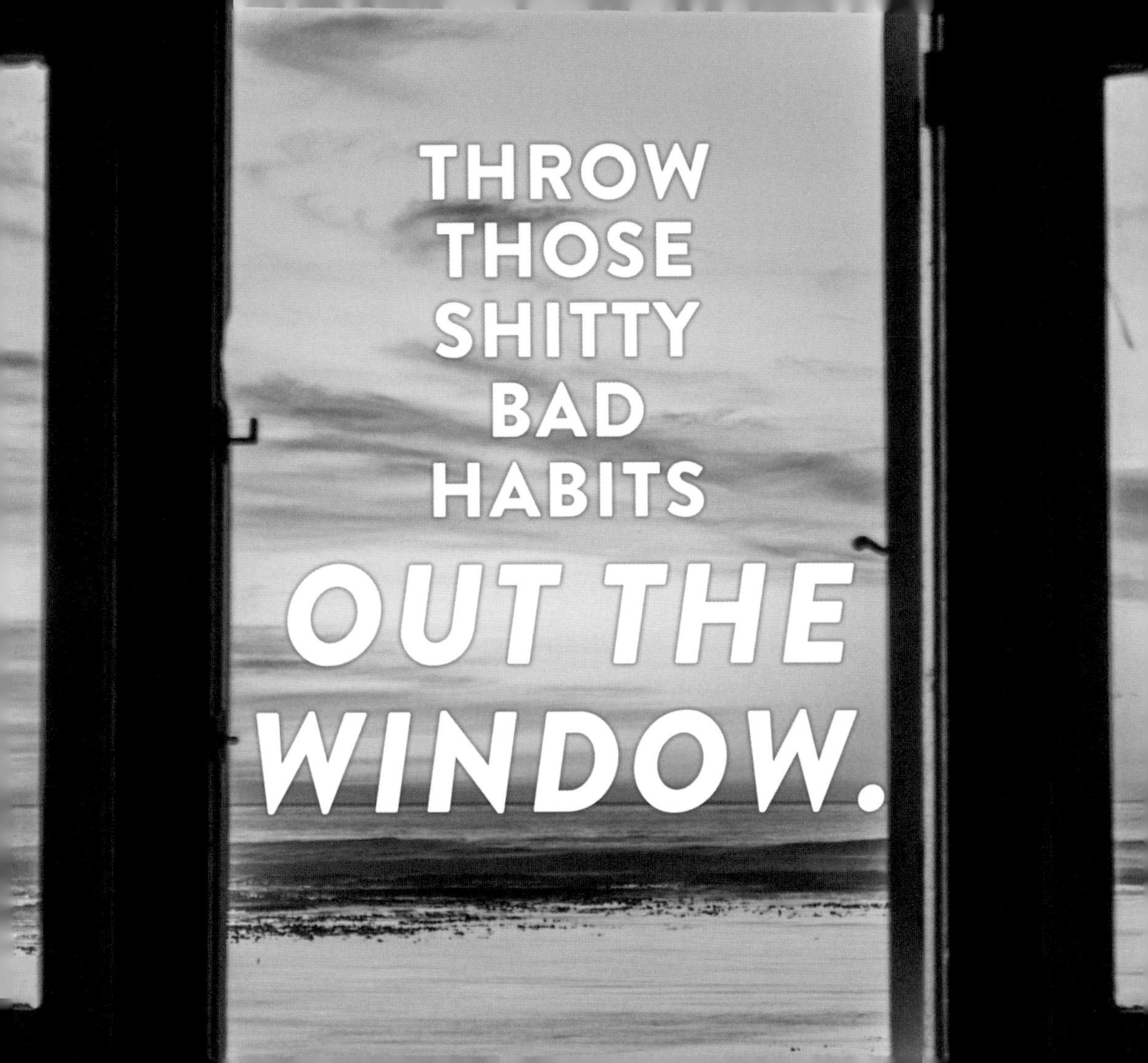
THROW
THOSE
SHITTY
BAD
HABITS
OUT THE
WINDOW.

*Bad habits just slow you down from becoming the **badass** you know you are.*

You don't need to race around the whole **goddamn** *day trying to get everything done.* **No one wants a half-assed project.**

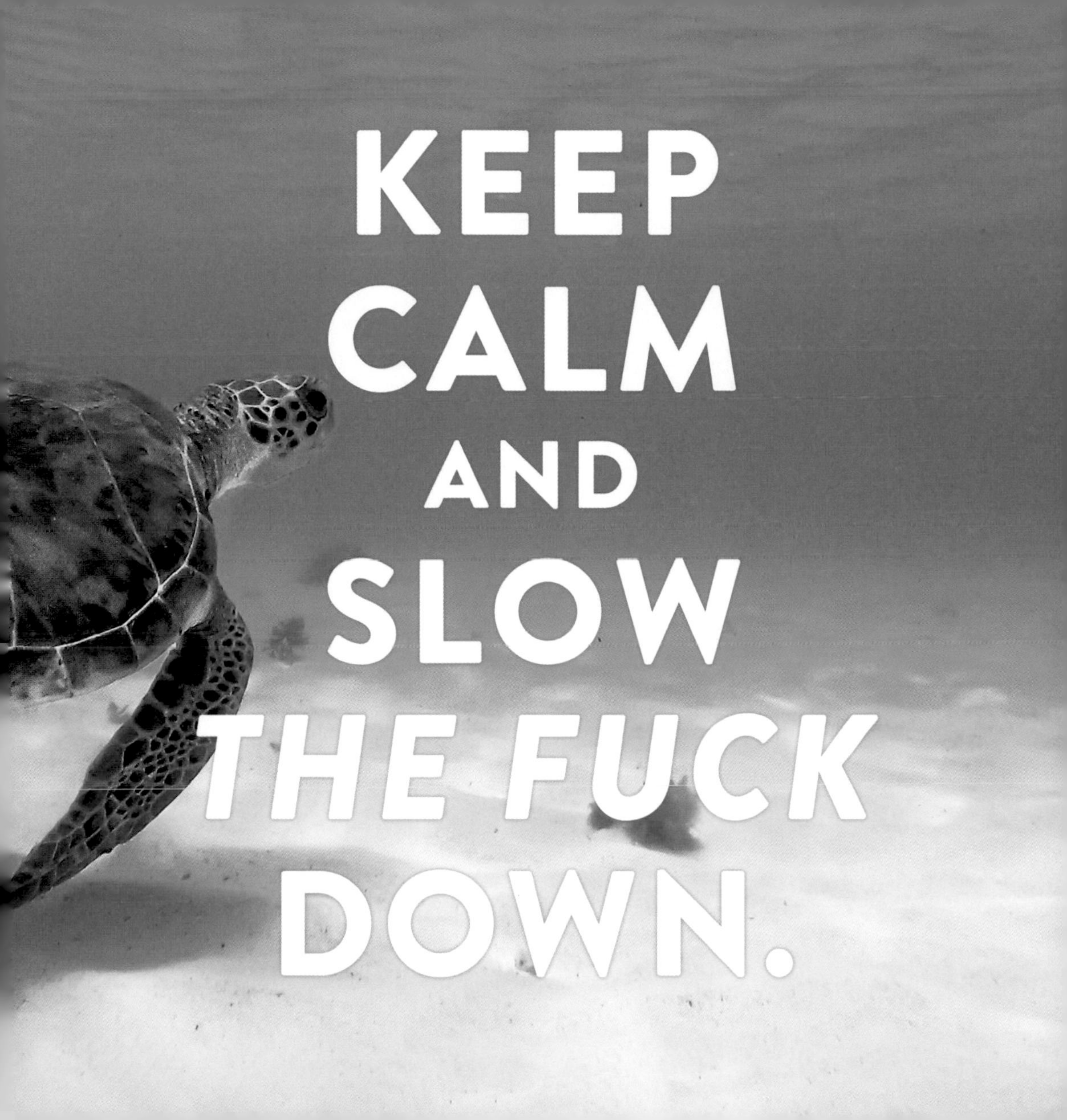
KEEP
CALM
AND
SLOW
THE FUCK
DOWN.

ACTIVATE YOUR BITCH MODE TODAY.

Today is the day to not take
any **shit from anyone.**

The only label you need right now is **Super Fucking Badass Bitch** who can handle whatever shit comes along.

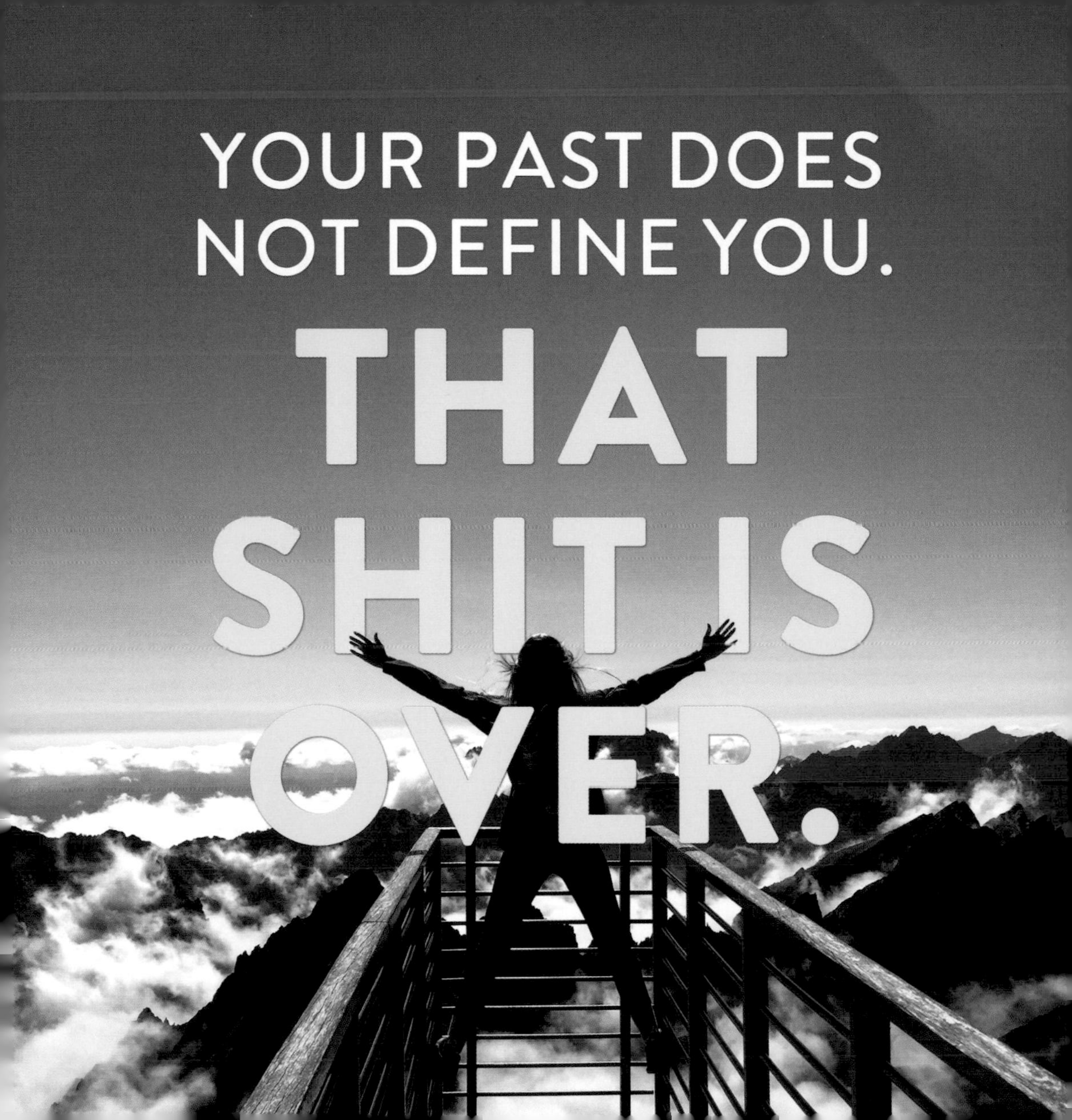
YOUR PAST DOES
NOT DEFINE YOU.
THAT
SHIT IS
OVER.

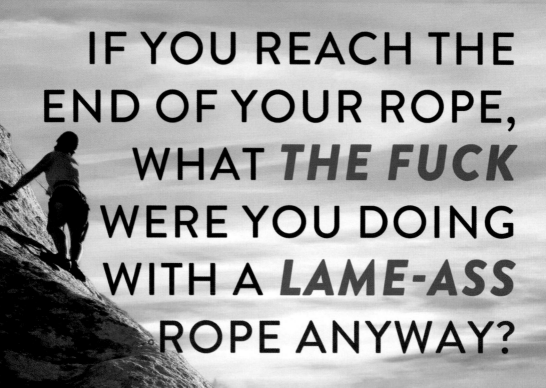

IF YOU REACH THE END OF YOUR ROPE, WHAT *THE FUCK* WERE YOU DOING WITH A *LAME-ASS* ROPE ANYWAY?

Yeah, some days are **fucking difficult.**

Find something strong to hang on to,

like your own damn courage.

*Those self-doubts don't stand a damn chance when you're in **bitch mode.***

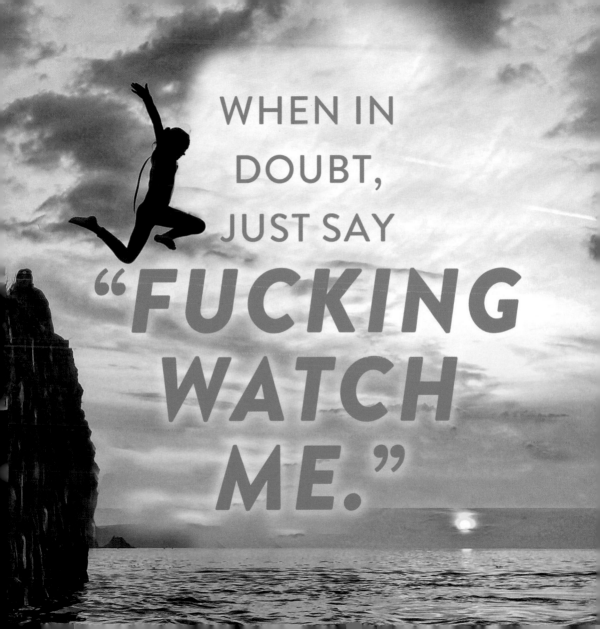

NEVER LIGHT A CANDLE
AT BOTH ENDS.
YOU'LL
BURN
YOUR
FUCKING
FINGERS.

Your power is awesome, and you know when
it's time to **step the fuck back** and take it easy.

Just imagine what **new shit** you
can learn without all the judgments,
quizzes, and deadlines.

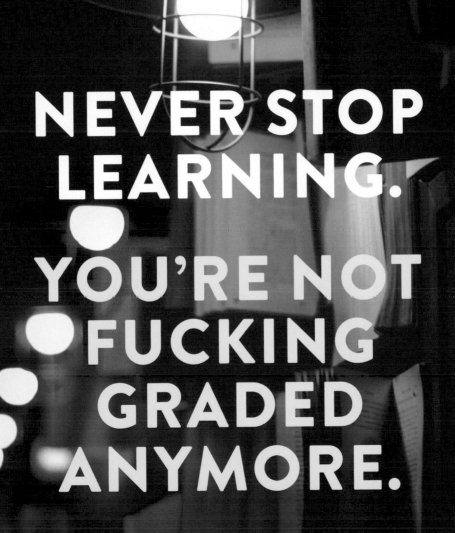

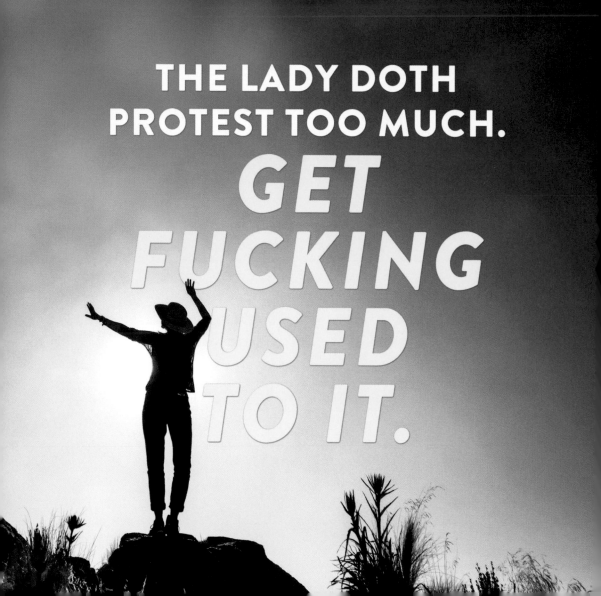

Sitting quietly and taking shit from others is so yesterday. *Let's hear that voice, bitch.*

You have the power to make your voice heard and leave a **fuck ton of gasps** in your wake.

TURN THOSE GODDAMN OBSTACLES INTO OPPORTUNITIES.

Whatever is messing up your plans,
*just **crush the fuck out of it***
and add it to your personal résumé.

Don't wait around to see if something good will happen. **Today is where it's fucking at.**

SEIZE *THE FUCK* OUT OF THIS DAY.

GOOD THINGS COME TO THOSE WHO DON'T
SIT AROUND ALL FUCKING DAY.

*There are so many **fucktastic joys** out there,*
so get off your ass and get one.

*Trying to make do with a bad situation is bullshit. Reject those lemons and **get some goddamn happy fruit** with ice cream.*

WHEN LIFE
GIVES YOU
LEMONS,
**THROW
THOSE DAMN
THINGS
BACK.**

BE THE HERO OF YOUR OWN DAMN STORY.

No one can live your damn life like you can,

*so take **charge of your own fucking chapters.***

*Whining about troubles and imagining the worst does no fucking good. Focus on the here and now and **all the good shit** that's happening today.*

THE BEST IS YET TO...

FUCK THAT.

IT'S ALREADY HERE.

WORRIES TAKE A BACK FUCKING SEAT TO TAKING CARE OF YOURSELF.

WTF

ARE YOU *DOING* OTHERWISE?

Get your priorities in line, bitch.
Worrying has **no damn place** in your day.

Congratu-fucking-lations on even trying something new. Get yourself a damn trophy and do it again.

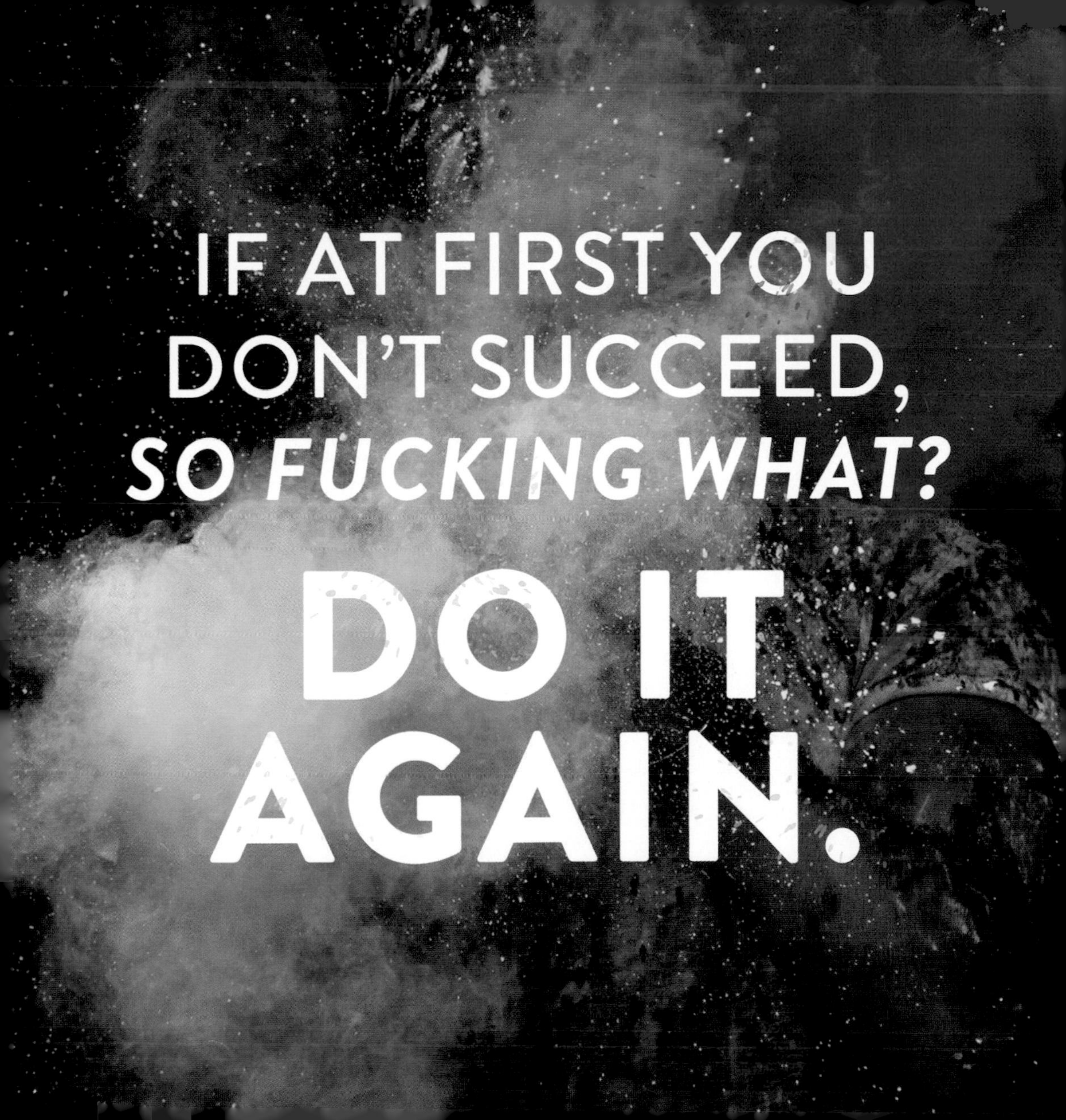
IF AT FIRST YOU
DON'T SUCCEED,
SO FUCKING WHAT?
DO IT
AGAIN.

LIFE'S A MARATHON. SO WHAT? YOU'VE GOT *BADASS* RUNNING SHOES.

*Even though the road looks long and exhausting, gather the shit you need, pack it up, and **blast the fuck** out of the starting gate.*

*Clear your damn calendar and **make a plan to not have a fucking plan.***

IF PLAN A OR B DOESN'T WORK,

MAYBE YOU DON'T NEED A GODDAMN PLAN.

YES, YOU DAMN WELL FUCKING CAN.

*That wishy-washy uncertainty is **bullshit.***
You know damn well you are capable.

*Dwelling on old mistakes won't get you a goddamn thing but a **headache.***

WHAT'S DONE IS DONE, SO MOVE THE FUCK ON.

THE ROAD TO SUCCESS IS PAVED WITH *YOUR FUCKING* COURAGE.

*Have gratitude for those who helped you along the way and especially for **your own fucking strength** in getting there.*

*Sit the fuck down to go over your dreams
and decide which one is next.*
You ain't got all year.

LIFE IS SHORT.

NO SHIT, SHERLOCK.

PERFECTION IS SO FUCKING OVERRATED.

You are exactly how you should be
this very fucking minute. **Stop listening to
assholes** who tell you otherwise.

It's okay to follow along to feel comfortable,
but veer off on your own damn road
every now and then.

TAKE THE ROAD LESS TRAVELED SO YOU DON'T STEP IN ANYONE'S SHIT.

WHEN OPPORTUNITY
COMES KNOCKING,

BAKE IT
GODDAMN
COOKIES.

Opportunity comes in all shapes and sizes,
*so learn to **recognize that shit** and take*
whatever comes your way.

TAKE A DEEP
BREATH,
THEN KEEP
FUCKING
SWIMMING.

*Giving up is not an option. Sit down for a minute if you have to, but **get the fuck back on the road.***

*Resting was nice. Now **get off your ass,** check off something from your to-do list, and **get your fucking star** for the day.*

TODAY IS THE FIRST DAY OF

THE REST OF YOUR GODDAMN TO-DO LIST.

THERE'S NO TIME FOR ANGER. TOO MUCH SHIT TO DO.

Anger will fuck up your mental health day.
Soothe that shit *and get back to life.*

TREAT OTHERS AS THE FUCKING STAR IN YOU DESERVES TO BE TREATED.

You are a rock star at being nice and respectful.
Go you! Now **demand the same shit**
from everyone else.

You may have a classy work mode, but never forget your **wild bitch self** who's always with you.

KEEP YOUR WILD ASS INTERNAL FONT ON BOLD.

MAY THE
FUCKING FIFTH,
SIXTH, AND
SEVENTH BE
WITH YOU TOO.

*Make **every goddamn day** count,*
not just special days on the calendar.

Asking for what you want isn't easy, but you sure as hell can try. **Let your goddamn voice be heard!**

ACTIONS SPEAK LOUDER THAN WORDS, BUT GO AHEAD AND

SCREAM ALL THE FUCK YOU WANT.

THE DARKEST HOUR *IS JUST* A GODDAMN TIME OF NIGHT.

*When things feel they are at their lowest, turn on **every fucking light** you can find.*

*You've done some good shit in your day and helped out a lot of people. Now sit back and feel how **fucking legendary** you are!*

DON'T PUT OFF TILL
TOMORROW UNLESS YOU
TOTALLY
FUCKING
FEEL
LIKE IT.

It's okay to set aside tasks and concentrate on your damn needs for the day. **Do what makes you happy right this fucking moment.**

DON'T SPEND TOO MUCH
TIME ON DECISIONS. SAY,
"WHAT
THE HELL,"
AND GET ON WITH IT.

*Overthinking decisions is a **fucking waste of time.** Get your ass moving and decide.*

Do what you need to do if it makes you happy. It's about goddamn time.

HAPPINESS IS A WARM PUPPY.
ADD WINE AND YOU'VE GOT
FUCKING BLISS.

LAUGHTER IS THE BEST MEDICINE,
SO TAKE A SPOONFUL OF

LAUGH YOUR ASS OFF
TWICE A DAY.

*Grin, giggle, and laugh **all the fuck you want.** If people start looking your way, maybe you've gone a little too fucking far.*

All those sunny days are great to show off your shiny self, so if a **fucking cloud or two gets in the way**, let out that inner radiance.

A DAY WITHOUT SUNSHINE IS NO BIG FUCKING DEAL BECAUSE YOU ARE ONE HELL OF A STAR.

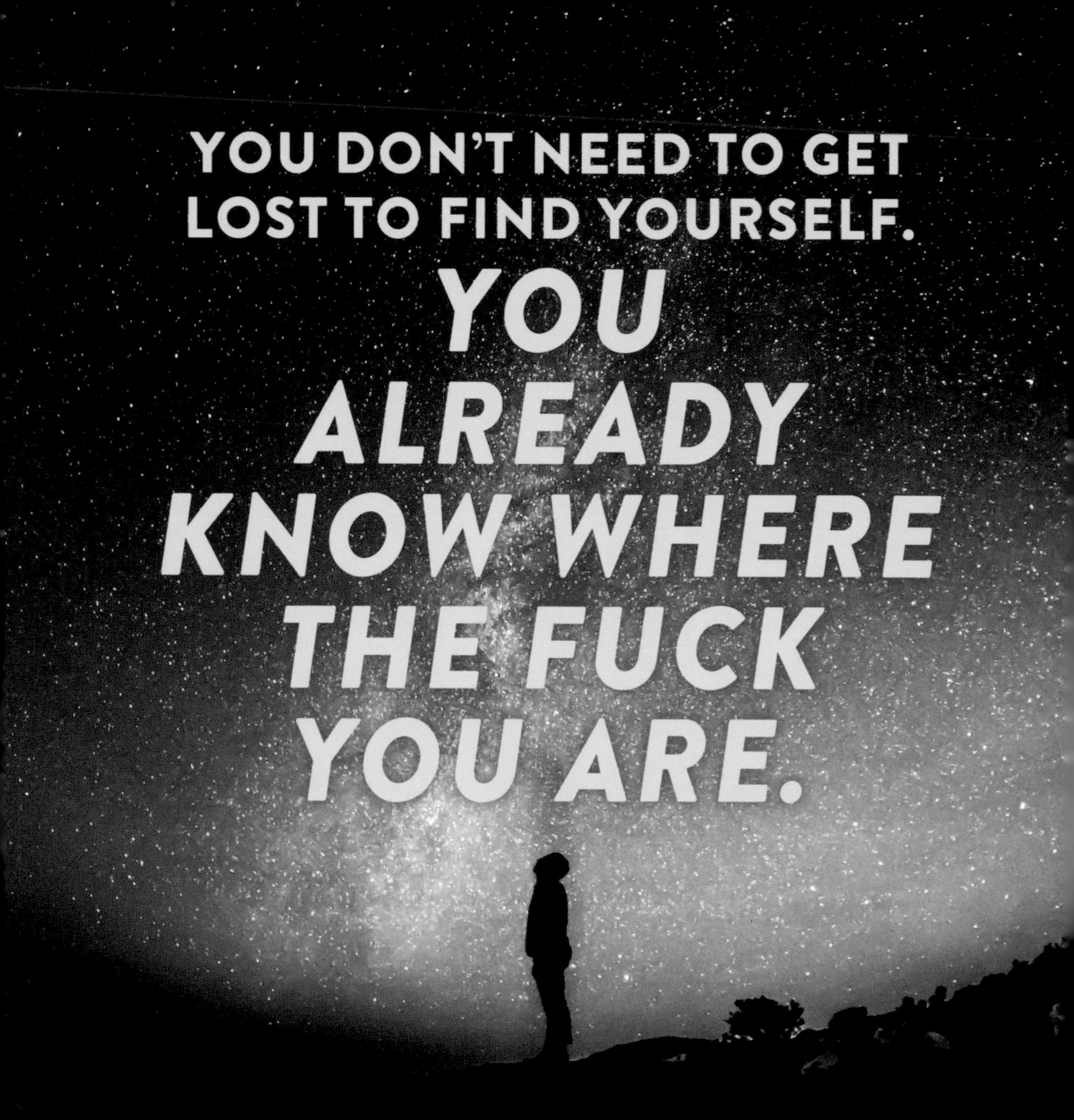
YOU DON'T NEED TO GET LOST TO FIND YOURSELF.
YOU ALREADY KNOW WHERE THE FUCK YOU ARE.

Detours are well and good, and searching
for your true self is fan-fucking-tastic.
But you already know where the hell you've
been and where you are going, so
embrace the you that is now.

You think you're too old or it's past time to start a new project? **Bullshit.** Get the fuck moving!

Fuck normal. Find the real you and
stand the fuck out in a crowd!

The road is long, fucking tiring sometimes, and you don't always get an updated map. Does that stop you? **Fuck no. Buckle the hell up!**

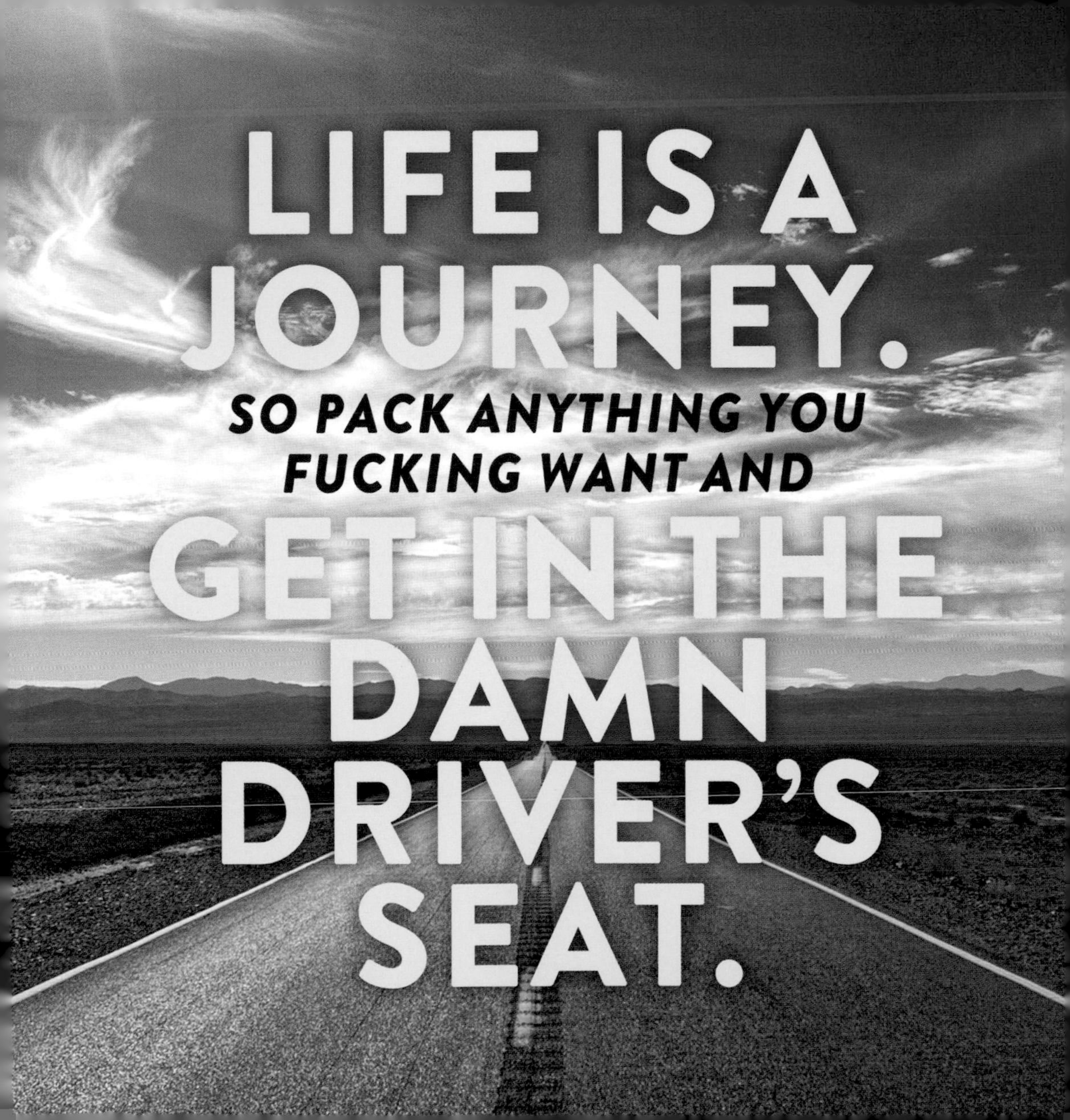
LIFE IS A JOURNEY.
SO PACK ANYTHING YOU FUCKING WANT AND
GET IN THE DAMN DRIVER'S SEAT.

IF YOU CAN'T SEE THE FOREST FOR THE TREES, THEN CLIMB ON SOMETHING AND USE YOUR **GODDAMN BINOCULARS.**

Trying to get a grasp on the big picture is fucking hard when so many damn little things get in the way. **Get a fucking different view.**

You don't need to take that shit and try to grow from every goddamn trauma. **Let it fucking go**, and get back on the road.

WHAT DOESN'T KILL YOU **HAD BETTER GET THE FUCK OUT OF YOUR WAY.**

TIME HEALS ALL WOUNDS.

MEDICAL ATTENTION ALSO HELPS.

Sometimes it's okay not to wait for mistakes to fade from your memory. Fix it now and **get it fucking over with.**

Who won't judge you for those fucked-up secrets and mistakes? You. **Fuck yeah.**

BE YOUR OWN BEST DAMN FRIEND.

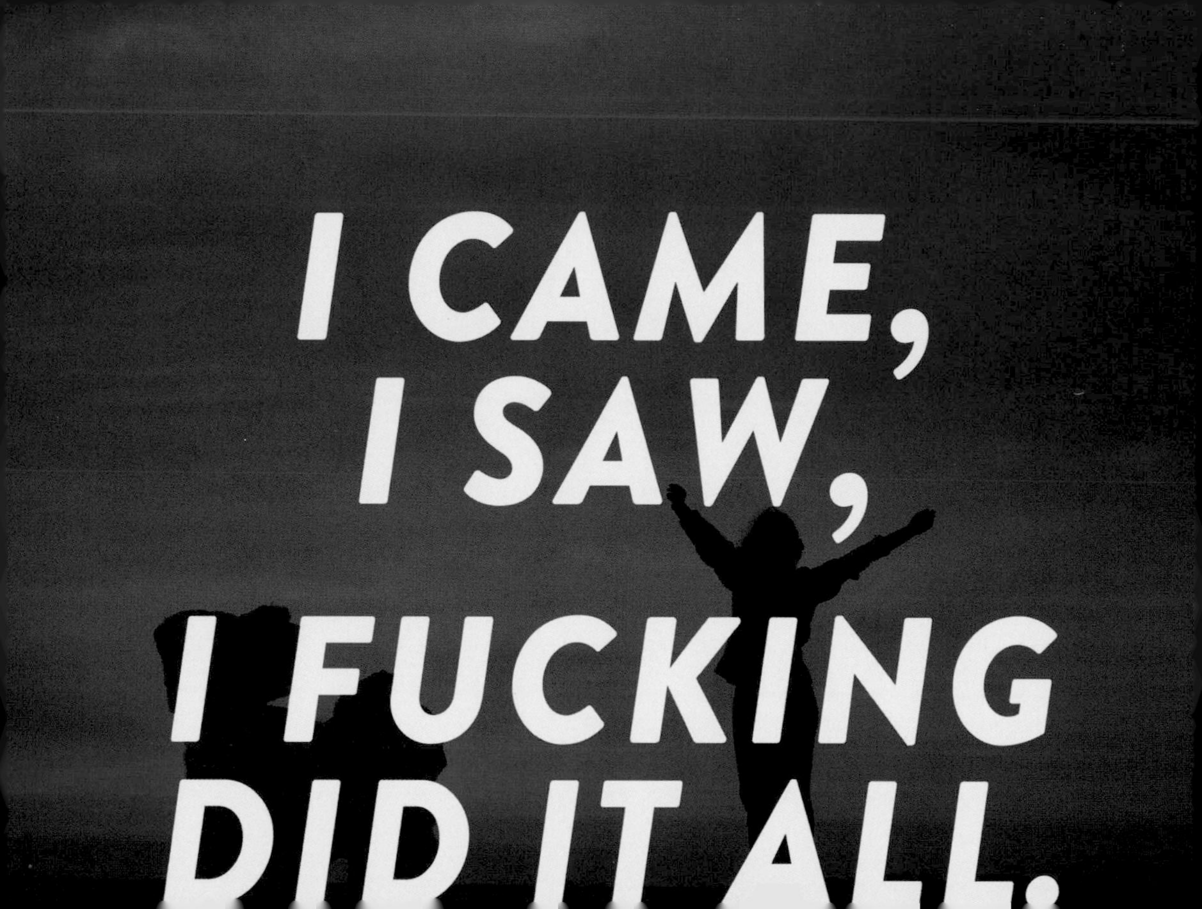
I CAME,
I SAW,
I FUCKING
DID IT ALL.

*Look at all you've accomplished this year. That's one hell of a list. It's **fucking amazing,** isn't it?*

You are in control of your own damn future,
so choose things that make you happy, and
any bad shit can **shut the fuck up!**

IT WAS THE
BEST OF
TIMES,
AND IT'S GOING TO
FUCKING STAY THE
BEST OF
TIMES.

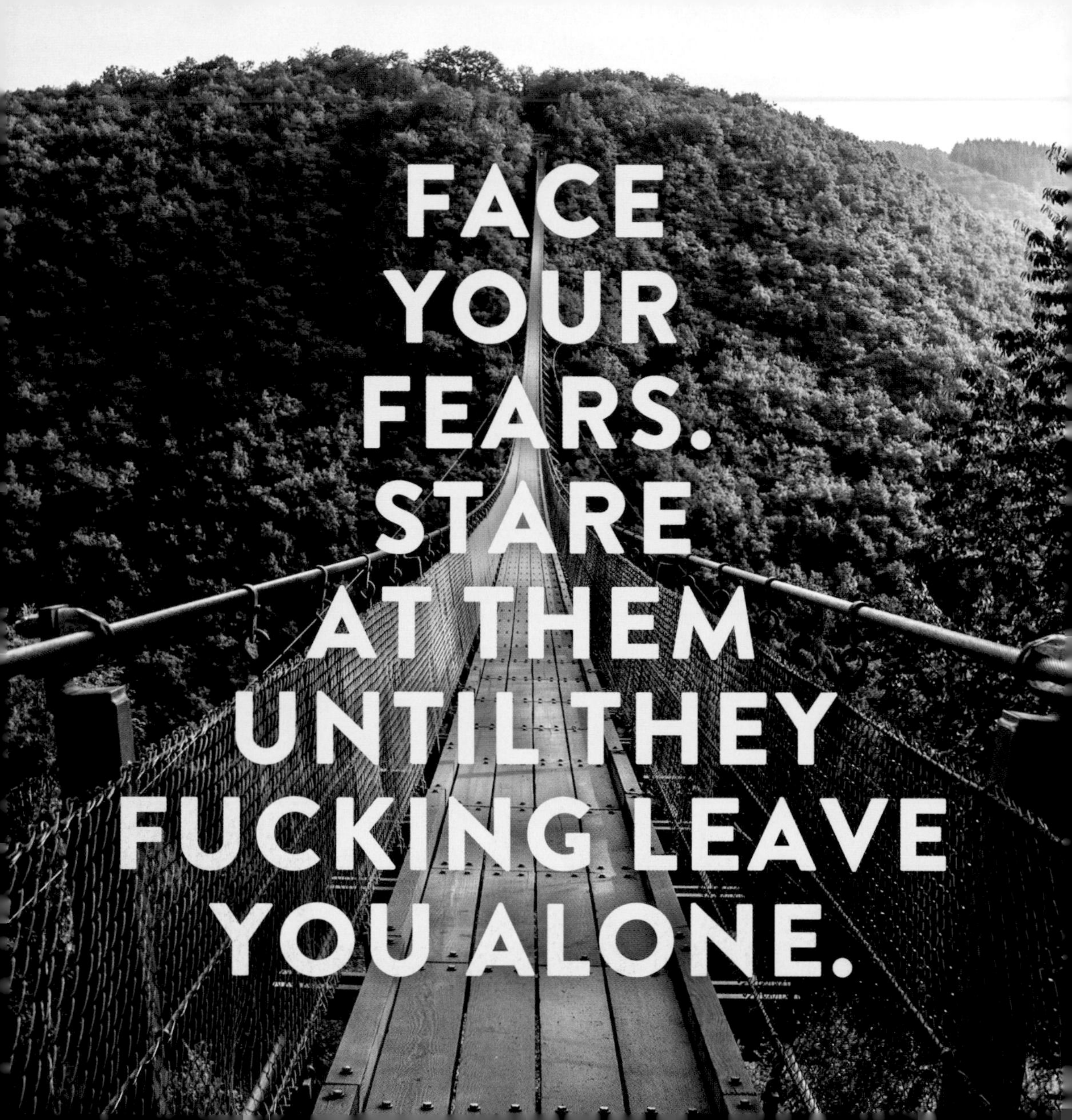
FACE
YOUR
FEARS.
STARE
AT THEM
UNTIL THEY
FUCKING LEAVE
YOU ALONE.

*Fuck fear. Look at it, **tell it to fuck off**, then go on your merry fucking way.*

*It's great to be prepared for shitty challenges. It's also great to be **first in the coffee line.***

EARLY TO BED,
EARLY TO RISE
WILL GET YOU
ALL THE
FUCKING
COFFEE.

It doesn't matter if you are in first or second place. **Celebrate your damn accomplishments** like the winner you are.

Doing things half-assed is not your style.
Go one step further, and who knows where
that extra mile will lead.

ALWAYS GO THE EXTRA MILE!

ONCE YOU'RE DONE YOU CAN GET **FUCKING ICE CREAM.**

WHAT'S IN A NAME? EVERYTHING, GODDAMNIT. MAKE YOURS KNOWN.

When you travel through life, don't forget to **make a fucking difference** in someone else's.

*You are in control of who makes you feel shitty or **fan-fucking-tastic.** Choose wisely!*

NO ONE CAN MAKE
YOU FEEL INFERIOR

ON ANY
FUCKING
DAY OF ANY
FUCKING
MONTH.

THERE'S NOTHING TO FEAR WHEN *YOU'RE A FUCKING BADASS.*

Take some fucked-up fear you've been holding and **shove that shit out the window.**

Sharing is caring, but first getting as much chocolate as you need is **caring for your own badass self.**

THE EARLY BIRD GETS *THE FUCKING CUPCAKE.*

ALL THE WORLD DOESN'T HAVE TO BE A GODDAMN STAGE.

Stop being who people think you should be.

You're fucking amazing just as you are.

All that running around to get everything done in one day is bullshit. **Don't miss the fucking awesome roses** *right in front of you.*

A CLUTTERED DESK IS A SIGN THAT YOU DESERVE A **FUCKING BREAK.**

You can only handle so much shit in one day. Sort through your mess before it gets out of hand, then **slowly back the fuck away.**

Get out there and learn shit. **Do your damn research.** The power surge is fucking awesome.

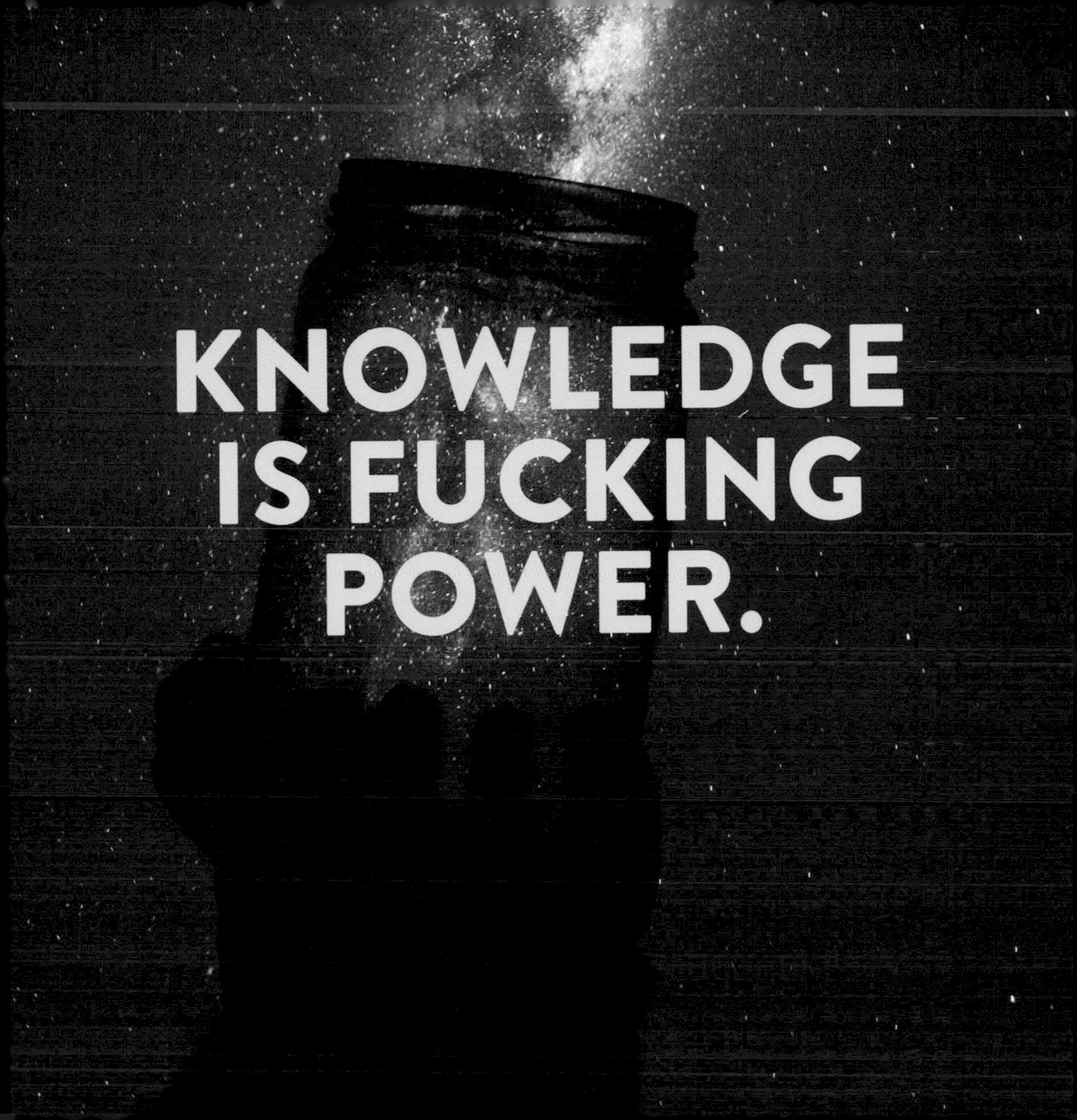
KNOWLEDGE
IS FUCKING
POWER.

DON'T BURN ALL YOUR BRIDGES. YOU MAY HAVE TO GO BACK AND WALK ACROSS THAT **HOT** SHIT.

*Yeah, some people are assholes. But you know who to keep in contact with and when to **run the fuck across the bridge** before it blows.*

Did you love learning in school? Good news! You can still learn as an adult, and you can learn **whatever the fuck you want.**

IGNORANCE IS *NOT FUCKING* BLISS. IT'S A **GODDAMN TRAGEDY.**

*There's nothing wrong with sitting a minute and not doing a damn thing. It's spiritual **re-fucking-juvenation.***

Don't be so **goddamn hard on yourself.**
Acknowledge the dumbass thing you did,
then give yourself all the comfort you need.

FORGIVE YOUR DAMN SELF.

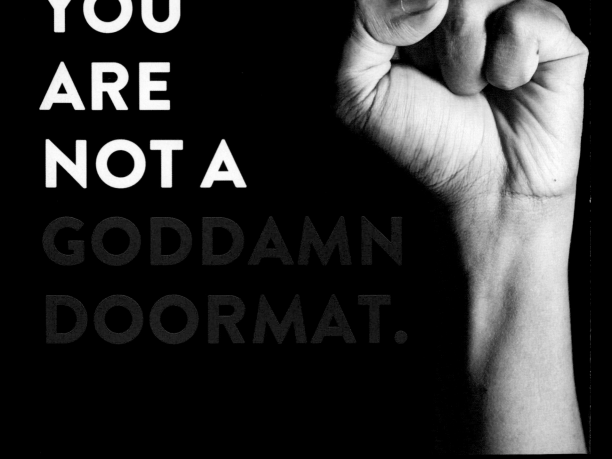

*Quiz: When is it okay for someone to walk the fuck all over you? Never. **Never fucking ever.***

*Do you have gullible written all over your face? Bitch, please. We all get taken in at one time or another. But **no fucking more.***

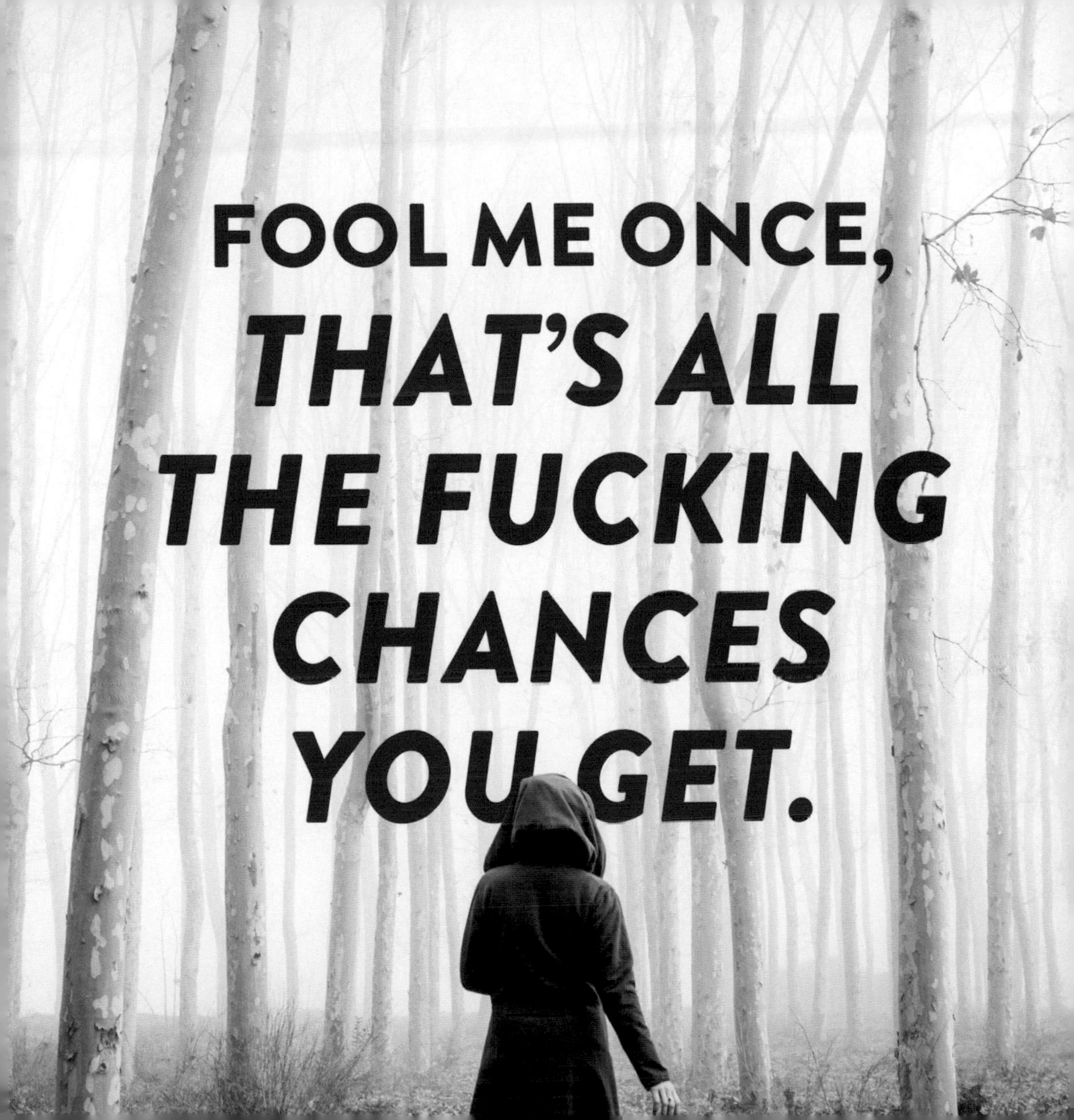
FOOL ME ONCE,
THAT'S ALL
THE FUCKING
CHANCES
YOU GET.

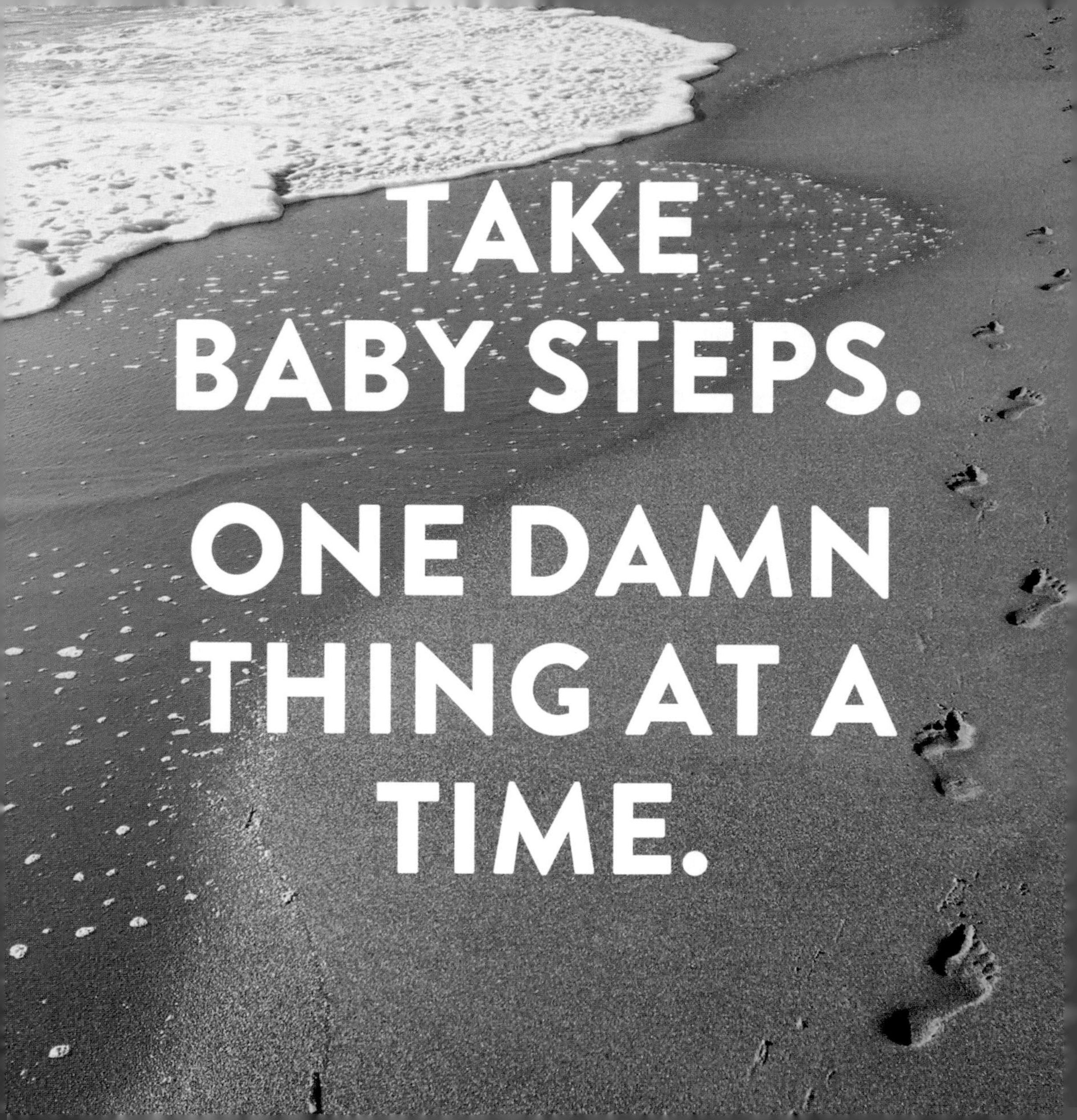
TAKE
BABY STEPS.
ONE DAMN
THING AT A
TIME.

Let all the **other fuckers fall over their feet** getting to the finish line.

Don't let fear hold you back. **Just fucking try.**

THERE'S NO STOPPING YOU.

NOT A FUCKING CHANCE.

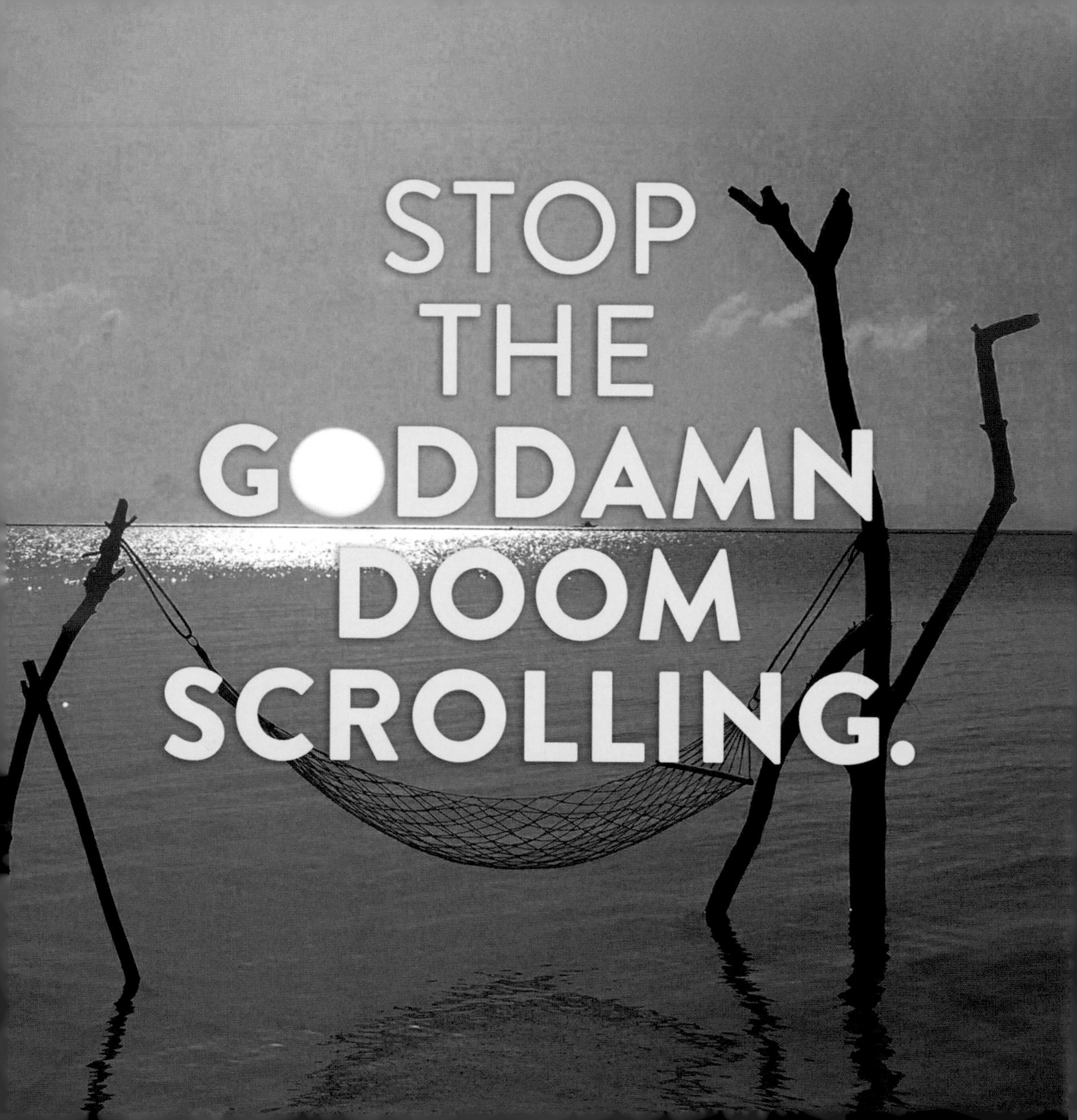
STOP
THE
GODDAMN
DOOM
SCROLLING.

Remember, social media is a breeding ground for assholes. Try putting the phone down for **just five fucking minutes.**

Repeat this right now: "I am enough, **no matter what those motherfuckers think.**"

DON'T LET THE ASSHOLES RAIN ON YOUR AFFIRMATION PARADE.

*News flash: You don't have to be good at something to enjoy and find value in it, regardless of what all the **bullshit** productivity culture says.*

GET OUT THERE AND SHOW THE FUCK OFF.